This House Hunting Journal Belongs To:

Trey & Kaitie ♡

ADDRESS *Information*

PREVIOUS ADDRESS:

REALTOR:

NAME:

AGENCY:

PHONE:

EMAIL:

CLOSING DATE:

DATE:

PREVIOUS ADDRESS:

REALTOR

NAME:

AGENCY:

PHONE:

EMAIL:

CLOSING DATE:

DATE:

NOTES & REMINDERS

IMPORTANT *Contacts*

CLOSING ATTORNEY

NAME:

ADDRESS:

✉ EMAIL:

📞 PHONE:

MORTGAGE BROKER / COMPANY

NAME:

ADDRESS:

✉ EMAIL:

📞 PHONE:

MOVING COMPANY

NAME:

ADDRESS:

✉ EMAIL:

📞 PHONE:

HOME APPRAISER

NAME:

ADDRESS:

✉ EMAIL:

📞 PHONE:

NOTES & REMINDERS

IMPORTANT Dates

MONTH:

NOTES & REMINDERS

PROPERTY INSPECTION
Checklist

EXTERIOR CONDITION:

GOOD   OK   BAD

- EXTERIOR OF PROPERTY
- FRONT DOOR
- PORCH/DECK/PATIO
- DRIVEWAY
- GARAGE DOORS
- OUTDOOR LIGHTING
- PAINT & TRIM
- WINDOWS
- WALKWAY

NOTES:

ROOF CONDITION:

GOOD   OK   BAD

- CHIMNEY
- GUTTERS & DOWNSPOUTS
- SOFITS & FASCIA
- YEAR ROOF WAS REPLACED:

NOTES:

GARAGE CONDITION:

GOOD   OK   BAD

- CEILING
- DOORS
- FLOORS & WALLS
- YEAR DOOR OPENERS WERE REPLACED:

NOTES:

YARD CONDITION:

GOOD   OK   BAD

- DRAINAGE
- FENCES & GATES
- RETAINING WALL
- SPRINKLER SYSTEM

NOTES:

PROPERTY INSPECTION
Checklist

OTHER IMPORTANT AREAS:	GOOD	OK	BAD	NOTES:
FOUNDATION				
MASONRY VENEERS				
EXTERIOR PAINT				
STORM WINDOWS				
PLUMBING				
ELECTRICAL OUTLETS				
FLOORING IN ROOMS				
WOOD TRIM				
FIREPLACE				

KITCHEN CONDITION:	GOOD	OK	BAD	NOTES:
WORKING EXHAUST FAN				
NO LEAKS IN PIPES				
APPLIANCES OPERATE				
OTHER:				

BATHROOM CONDITION:	GOOD	OK	BAD	NOTES:
PROPER DRAINAGE				
NO LEAKS IN PIPES				
CAULKING IN GOOD SHAPE				
TILES ARE SECURE				

MISC:	GOOD	OK	BAD	NOTES:
SMOKE & CARBON DETECTORS				
STAIRWAY TREADS SOLID				
STAIR HANDRAILS INSTALLED				
OTHER:				
OTHER:				
OTHER:				

HOUSE HUNTING *List*

ADDRESS		

HOUSE HUNTING *List*

ADDRESS		

HOUSE HUNTING *List*

ADDRESS		

HOUSE HUNTING *List*

ADDRESS		

HOUSE HUNTING *List*

ADDRESS		

HOUSE HUNTING *List*

ADDRESS		

HOUSE HUNTING *List*

ADDRESS		

HOUSE HUNTING *List*

ADDRESS		

HOUSE HUNTING *List*

ADDRESS

HOUSE HUNTING *List*

ADDRESS		

HOUSE HUNTING
Checklist

HOUSE SCORE:

PROPERTY ADDRESS

ASKING PRICE:

PROPERTY TAXES:

LOT SIZE:

PROPERTY SIZE:

FINISH:
- BRICK
- WOOD
- STUCCO
- SIDING

AGE OF PROPERTY:

NEIGHBORHOOD

DISTANCE TO SCHOOLS:

DISTANCE TO WORK:

PUBLIC TRANSPORTATION:

MEDICAL:

RECREATION:

SHOPPING:

ADDITIONAL INFO:

NOTES:

HOUSE HUNTING *Checklist*

DETAILED HOUSE FEATURES:

OF BEDROOMS: # OF BATHROOMS:

BASEMENT: HEATING TYPE:

PROPERTY CHECKLIST:

POOL ☐	BONUS ROOM ☐	NOTES	
GARAGE ☐	LAUNDRY CHUTE ☐		
FIREPLACE ☐	FENCED YARD ☐		
EN-SUITE ☐	APPLIANCES ☐		
OFFICE ☐	A/C ☐		
DECK ☐	HEAT PUMP ☐		

PARKING ☐

CLOSETS ☐

STORAGE ☐

☐

☐

☐

☐

☐

☐

☐

NOTES

HOUSE HUNTING
Checklist

HOUSE SCORE:

PROPERTY ADDRESS

ASKING PRICE:

PROPERTY TAXES:

LOT SIZE:

PROPERTY SIZE:

FINISH:
- [ ] BRICK
- [ ] STUCCO
- [ ] WOOD
- [ ] SIDING

AGE OF PROPERTY:

NEIGHBORHOOD

DISTANCE TO SCHOOLS:

DISTANCE TO WORK:

PUBLIC TRANSPORTATION:

MEDICAL:

RECREATION:

SHOPPING:

ADDITIONAL INFO:

NOTES:

HOUSE HUNTING *Checklist*

DETAILED HOUSE FEATURES:

OF BEDROOMS:

OF BATHROOMS:

BASEMENT:

HEATING TYPE:

PROPERTY CHECKLIST:

POOL	☐		BONUS ROOM	☐	NOTES
GARAGE	☐		LAUNDRY CHUTE	☐	
FIREPLACE	☐		FENCED YARD	☐	
EN-SUITE	☐		APPLIANCES	☐	
OFFICE	☐		A/C	☐	
DECK	☐		HEAT PUMP	☐	

PARKING	☐	NOTES
CLOSETS	☐	
STORAGE	☐	
	☐	
	☐	
	☐	
	☐	
	☐	
	☐	
	☐	

HOUSE HUNTING
Checklist

HOUSE SCORE:

PROPERTY ADDRESS

ASKING PRICE:

PROPERTY TAXES:

LOT SIZE:

PROPERTY SIZE:

FINISH:
- BRICK
- STUCCO
- WOOD
- SIDING

AGE OF PROPERTY:

NEIGHBORHOOD

DISTANCE TO SCHOOLS:

DISTANCE TO WORK:

PUBLIC TRANSPORTATION:

MEDICAL:

RECREATION:

SHOPPING:

ADDITIONAL INFO:

NOTES:

HOUSE HUNTING *Checklist*

DETAILED HOUSE FEATURES:

OF BEDROOMS: # OF BATHROOMS:

BASEMENT: HEATING TYPE:

PROPERTY CHECKLIST:

POOL	☐	BONUS ROOM	☐	NOTES
GARAGE	☐	LAUNDRY CHUTE	☐	
FIREPLACE	☐	FENCED YARD	☐	
EN-SUITE	☐	APPLIANCES	☐	
OFFICE	☐	A/C	☐	
DECK	☐	HEAT PUMP	☐	

PARKING	☐	NOTES
CLOSETS	☐	
STORAGE	☐	

HOUSE HUNTING
Checklist

HOUSE SCORE:

PROPERTY ADDRESS

ASKING PRICE:

PROPERTY TAXES:

LOT SIZE:

PROPERTY SIZE:

FINISH:
- [ ] BRICK
- [ ] STUCCO
- [ ] WOOD
- [ ] SIDING

AGE OF PROPERTY:

NEIGHBORHOOD

DISTANCE TO SCHOOLS:

DISTANCE TO WORK:

PUBLIC TRANSPORTATION:

MEDICAL:

RECREATION:

SHOPPING:

ADDITIONAL INFO:

NOTES:

HOUSE HUNTING *Checklist*

DETAILED HOUSE FEATURES:

OF BEDROOMS: # OF BATHROOMS:

BASEMENT: HEATING TYPE:

PROPERTY CHECKLIST:

POOL	☐		BONUS ROOM	☐		NOTES
GARAGE	☐		LAUNDRY CHUTE	☐		
FIREPLACE	☐		FENCED YARD	☐		
EN-SUITE	☐		APPLIANCES	☐		
OFFICE	☐		A/C	☐		
DECK	☐		HEAT PUMP	☐		

PARKING ☐
CLOSETS ☐
STORAGE ☐
☐
☐
☐
☐
☐
☐
☐

NOTES

HOUSE HUNTING
Checklist

HOUSE SCORE:

PROPERTY ADDRESS

ASKING PRICE:

PROPERTY TAXES:

LOT SIZE:

PROPERTY SIZE:

FINISH:
- [ ] BRICK
- [ ] STUCCO
- [ ] WOOD
- [ ] SIDING

AGE OF PROPERTY:

NEIGHBORHOOD

DISTANCE TO SCHOOLS:

DISTANCE TO WORK:

PUBLIC TRANSPORTATION:

MEDICAL:

RECREATION:

SHOPPING:

ADDITIONAL INFO:

NOTES:

HOUSE HUNTING *Checklist*

DETAILED HOUSE FEATURES:

OF BEDROOMS: # OF BATHROOMS:

BASEMENT: HEATING TYPE:

PROPERTY CHECKLIST:

POOL	☐
GARAGE	☐
FIREPLACE	☐
EN-SUITE	☐
OFFICE	☐
DECK	☐

BONUS ROOM	☐
LAUNDRY CHUTE	☐
FENCED YARD	☐
APPLIANCES	☐
A/C	☐
HEAT PUMP	☐

NOTES

PARKING	☐
CLOSETS	☐
STORAGE	☐
	☐
	☐
	☐
	☐
	☐
	☐

NOTES

HOUSE HUNTING
Checklist

HOUSE SCORE:

PROPERTY ADDRESS

ASKING PRICE:

PROPERTY TAXES:

LOT SIZE:

PROPERTY SIZE:

FINISH:

☐ BRICK ☐ STUCCO

☐ WOOD ☐ SIDING

AGE OF PROPERTY:

NEIGHBORHOOD

DISTANCE TO SCHOOLS:

DISTANCE TO WORK:

PUBLIC TRANSPORTATION:

MEDICAL:

RECREATION:

SHOPPING:

ADDITIONAL INFO:

NOTES:

HOUSE HUNTING *Checklist*

DETAILED HOUSE FEATURES:

OF BEDROOMS: # OF BATHROOMS:

BASEMENT: HEATING TYPE:

PROPERTY CHECKLIST:

POOL	☐	BONUS ROOM	☐	NOTES
GARAGE	☐	LAUNDRY CHUTE	☐	
FIREPLACE	☐	FENCED YARD	☐	
EN-SUITE	☐	APPLIANCES	☐	
OFFICE	☐	A/C	☐	
DECK	☐	HEAT PUMP	☐	

PARKING	☐	NOTES
CLOSETS	☐	
STORAGE	☐	
	☐	
	☐	
	☐	
	☐	
	☐	
	☐	
	☐	

HOUSE HUNTING
Checklist

HOUSE SCORE:

PROPERTY ADDRESS

ASKING PRICE:

PROPERTY TAXES:

LOT SIZE:

PROPERTY SIZE:

FINISH:
- [ ] BRICK
- [ ] STUCCO
- [ ] WOOD
- [ ] SIDING

AGE OF PROPERTY:

NEIGHBORHOOD

DISTANCE TO SCHOOLS:

DISTANCE TO WORK:

PUBLIC TRANSPORTATION:

MEDICAL:

RECREATION:

SHOPPING:

ADDITIONAL INFO:

NOTES:

HOUSE HUNTING *Checklist*

DETAILED HOUSE FEATURES:

OF BEDROOMS: # OF BATHROOMS:

BASEMENT: HEATING TYPE:

PROPERTY CHECKLIST:

POOL	☐		BONUS ROOM	☐	NOTES
GARAGE	☐		LAUNDRY CHUTE	☐	
FIREPLACE	☐		FENCED YARD	☐	
EN-SUITE	☐		APPLIANCES	☐	
OFFICE	☐		A/C	☐	
DECK	☐		HEAT PUMP	☐	

PARKING	☐	NOTES
CLOSETS	☐	
STORAGE	☐	
	☐	
	☐	
	☐	
	☐	
	☐	
	☐	
	☐	

HOUSE HUNTING
Checklist

HOUSE SCORE:

PROPERTY ADDRESS

ASKING PRICE:

PROPERTY TAXES:

LOT SIZE:

PROPERTY SIZE:

FINISH:
- [ ] BRICK
- [ ] STUCCO
- [ ] WOOD
- [ ] SIDING

AGE OF PROPERTY:

NEIGHBORHOOD

DISTANCE TO SCHOOLS:

DISTANCE TO WORK:

PUBLIC TRANSPORTATION:

MEDICAL:

RECREATION:

SHOPPING:

ADDITIONAL INFO:

NOTES:

HOUSE HUNTING *Checklist*

DETAILED HOUSE FEATURES:

OF BEDROOMS: # OF BATHROOMS:

BASEMENT: HEATING TYPE:

PROPERTY CHECKLIST:

POOL	☐	BONUS ROOM	☐	NOTES
GARAGE	☐	LAUNDRY CHUTE	☐	
FIREPLACE	☐	FENCED YARD	☐	
EN-SUITE	☐	APPLIANCES	☐	
OFFICE	☐	A/C	☐	
DECK	☐	HEAT PUMP	☐	

PARKING	☐	NOTES
CLOSETS	☐	
STORAGE	☐	

HOUSE HUNTING
Checklist

HOUSE SCORE:

PROPERTY ADDRESS

ASKING PRICE:

PROPERTY TAXES:

LOT SIZE:

PROPERTY SIZE:

FINISH:
- ☐ BRICK
- ☐ STUCCO
- ☐ WOOD
- ☐ SIDING

AGE OF PROPERTY:

NEIGHBORHOOD

DISTANCE TO SCHOOLS:

DISTANCE TO WORK:

PUBLIC TRANSPORTATION:

MEDICAL:

RECREATION:

SHOPPING:

ADDITIONAL INFO:

NOTES:

HOUSE HUNTING *Checklist*

DETAILED HOUSE FEATURES:

OF BEDROOMS: # OF BATHROOMS:

BASEMENT: HEATING TYPE:

PROPERTY CHECKLIST:

POOL	☐
GARAGE	☐
FIREPLACE	☐
EN-SUITE	☐
OFFICE	☐
DECK	☐

BONUS ROOM	☐
LAUNDRY CHUTE	☐
FENCED YARD	☐
APPLIANCES	☐
A/C	☐
HEAT PUMP	☐

NOTES

PARKING	☐
CLOSETS	☐
STORAGE	☐
	☐
	☐
	☐
	☐
	☐
	☐
	☐

NOTES

HOUSE HUNTING
Checklist

HOUSE SCORE:

PROPERTY ADDRESS

ASKING PRICE:

PROPERTY TAXES:

LOT SIZE:

PROPERTY SIZE:

FINISH:
- [ ] BRICK
- [ ] STUCCO
- [ ] WOOD
- [ ] SIDING

AGE OF PROPERTY:

NEIGHBORHOOD

DISTANCE TO SCHOOLS:

DISTANCE TO WORK:

PUBLIC TRANSPORTATION:

MEDICAL:

RECREATION:

SHOPPING:

ADDITIONAL INFO:

NOTES:

HOUSE HUNTING *Checklist*

DETAILED HOUSE FEATURES:

OF BEDROOMS: # OF BATHROOMS:

BASEMENT: HEATING TYPE:

PROPERTY CHECKLIST:

POOL	☐	BONUS ROOM	☐	NOTES
GARAGE	☐	LAUNDRY CHUTE	☐	
FIREPLACE	☐	FENCED YARD	☐	
EN-SUITE	☐	APPLIANCES	☐	
OFFICE	☐	A/C	☐	
DECK	☐	HEAT PUMP	☐	

PARKING	☐	NOTES
CLOSETS	☐	
STORAGE	☐	
	☐	
	☐	
	☐	
	☐	
	☐	
	☐	
	☐	

HOUSE HUNTING
Checklist

HOUSE SCORE:

PROPERTY ADDRESS

ASKING PRICE:

PROPERTY TAXES:

LOT SIZE:

PROPERTY SIZE:

FINISH:
- ☐ BRICK
- ☐ STUCCO
- ☐ WOOD
- ☐ SIDING

AGE OF PROPERTY:

NEIGHBORHOOD

DISTANCE TO SCHOOLS:

DISTANCE TO WORK:

PUBLIC TRANSPORTATION:

MEDICAL:

RECREATION:

SHOPPING:

ADDITIONAL INFO:

NOTES:

HOUSE HUNTING *Checklist*

DETAILED HOUSE FEATURES:

OF BEDROOMS: # OF BATHROOMS:

BASEMENT: HEATING TYPE:

PROPERTY CHECKLIST:

POOL	☐	BONUS ROOM	☐	NOTES
GARAGE	☐	LAUNDRY CHUTE	☐	
FIREPLACE	☐	FENCED YARD	☐	
EN-SUITE	☐	APPLIANCES	☐	
OFFICE	☐	A/C	☐	
DECK	☐	HEAT PUMP	☐	

PARKING	☐	NOTES
CLOSETS	☐	
STORAGE	☐	
	☐	
	☐	
	☐	
	☐	
	☐	
	☐	

House Hunting NOTES

House Hunting NOTES

House Hunting NOTES

House Hunting NOTES

House Hunting NOTES

House Hunting NOTES

House Hunting NOTES

House Hunting NOTES

House Hunting NOTES

House Hunting NOTES

House Hunting NOTES

BUDGET & *Expenses*

PREVIOUS RESIDENCE

EXPENSES	BUDGET	ACTUAL	DIFFERENCE

NEW RESIDENCE

EXPENSES	BUDGET	ACTUAL	DIFFERENCE

OTHER

EXPENSES	BUDGET	ACTUAL	DIFFERENCE

BUDGET & Expenses

PREVIOUS RESIDENCE

EXPENSES	BUDGET	ACTUAL	DIFFERENCE

NEW RESIDENCE

EXPENSES	BUDGET	ACTUAL	DIFFERENCE

OTHER

EXPENSES	BUDGET	ACTUAL	DIFFERENCE

BUDGET & *Expenses*

PREVIOUS RESIDENCE

EXPENSES	BUDGET	ACTUAL	DIFFERENCE

NEW RESIDENCE

EXPENSES	BUDGET	ACTUAL	DIFFERENCE

OTHER

EXPENSES	BUDGET	ACTUAL	DIFFERENCE

TO DO: *Previous Residence*

DATE:

MOST IMPORTANT

NOTES:

TO DO: *New Residence*

MOST IMPORTANT

NOTES:

TO DO: *New Residence*

MOST IMPORTANT

NOTES:

MOVING DAY *Planner*

PRIORITIES

MOVING DAY SCHEDULE

6 AM	
7 AM	
8 AM	
9 AM	
10 AM	
11 AM	
12 PM	
1 PM	
2 PM	
3 PM	
4 PM	
5 PM	
6 PM	
7 PM	
8 PM	
9 PM	
10 PM	
11 PM	
12 AM	

MOVING DAY TO DO LIST

ORGANIZATION

REMINDERS

MOVING DAY *List*

MOVING DAY *List*

OLD RESIDENCE	NEW RESIDENCE

MOVING DAY *List*

OLD RESIDENCE	NEW RESIDENCE

MOVING DAY *List*

OLD RESIDENCE	NEW RESIDENCE

Packing NOTES

Packing NOTES

Packing NOTES

ADDRESS CHANGE
Checklist

UTILITIES:

ELECTRIC

CABLE/SATELLITE

GAS

SECURITY SYSTEM

PHONE

INTERNET

WATER/SEWER

FINANCIAL:

BANK

CREDIT CARD

BANK STATEMENTS

EMPLOYER

INSURANCE

START/STOP *Utilities*

ELECTRIC COMPANY

NAME

PHONE

WEBSITE URL

START DATE

STOP DATE

ACCOUNT NUMBER

CABLE / SATELLITE

NAME

PHONE

WEBSITE URL

START DATE

STOP DATE

ACCOUNT NUMBER

GAS / HEATING COMPANY

NAME

PHONE

WEBSITE URL

START DATE

STOP DATE

ACCOUNT NUMBER

START/STOP *Utilities*

INTERNET PROVIDER

NAME

PHONE

WEBSITE URL

START DATE

STOP DATE

ACCOUNT NUMBER

SECURITY SYSTEM

NAME

PHONE

WEBSITE URL

START DATE

STOP DATE

ACCOUNT NUMBER

OTHER:

NAME

PHONE

WEBSITE URL

START DATE

STOP DATE

ACCOUNT NUMBER

NOTES:

NEW PROVIDER *Contacts*

MEDICAL

FAMILY DOCTOR

NAME:

PHONE:

EMAIL:

ADDRESS:

WEBSITE URL:

DENTIST

NAME:

PHONE:

EMAIL:

ADDRESS:

WEBSITE URL:

PEDIATRICIAN

NAME:

PHONE:

EMAIL:
ADDRESS:

WEBSITE URL:

NOTES

NEW PROVIDER *Contacts*

EDUCATION

SCHOOL #1:

NAME:

PHONE:

EMAIL:

ADDRESS:

WEBSITE URL:

SCHOOL #2:

NAME:

PHONE:

EMAIL:

ADDRESS:

WEBSITE URL:

SCHOOL #3:

NAME:

PHONE:

EMAIL:

ADDRESS:

WEBSITE URL:

NOTES

MOVING DAY *Planner*

6-WEEKS PRIOR

- [ ] HIRE A MOVING COMPANY
- [ ] KEEP RECEIPTS FOR TAX PURPOSES
- [ ] DETERMINE A BUDGET FOR MOVING EXPENSES
- [ ] ORGANIZE INVENTORY
- [ ] GET PACKING BOXES & LABELS
- [ ] PURGE / GIVE AWAY / SELL UNWANTED ITEMS
- [ ] CREATE AN INVENTORY SHEET OF ITEMS & BOXES
- [ ] RESEARCH SCHOOLS FOR YOUR CHILDREN
- [ ] PLAN A GARAGE SALE TO UNLOAD UNWANTED ITEMS

4-WEEKS PRIOR

- [ ] CONFIRM DATES WITH MOVING COMPANY
- [ ] RESEARCH YOUR NEW COMMUNITY
- [ ] START PACKING BOXES
- [ ] PURCHASE MOVING INSURANCE
- [ ] ORGANIZE FINANCIAL & LEGAL DOCUMENTS IN ONE PLACE
- [ ] FIND SNOW REMOVAL OR LANDSCAPE SERVICE FOR NEW RESIDENCE
- [ ] RESEARCH NEW DOCTOR, DENTIST, VETERNARIAN, ETC

2-WEEKS PRIOR

- [ ] PLAN FOR PET TRANSPORT DURING MOVE
- [ ] SET UP MAIL FORWARDING SERVICE
- [ ] TRANSFER HOMEOWNERS INSURANCE TO NEW RESIDENCE
- [ ] TRANSFER UTILITIES TO NEW RESIDENCE
- [ ] UPDATE YOUR DRIVER'S LICENSE

MOVING DAY *Planner*

6-WEEKS PRIOR

- [ ]
- [ ]
- [ ]
- [ ]
- [ ]
- [ ]
- [ ]
- [ ]
- [ ]

4-WEEKS PRIOR

- [ ]
- [ ]
- [ ]
- [ ]
- [ ]
- [ ]
- [ ]

2-WEEKS PRIOR

- [ ]
- [ ]
- [ ]
- [ ]
- [ ]

MOVING DAY *Planner*

WEEK OF MOVE

- [ ]
- [ ]
- [ ]
- [ ]
- [ ]
- [ ]
- [ ]
- [ ]

MOVING DAY

- [ ]
- [ ]
- [ ]
- [ ]
- [ ]
- [ ]

NOTES & REMINDERS

MOVING DAY *Planner*

6-WEEKS PRIOR

- [ ]
- [ ]
- [ ]
- [ ]
- [ ]
- [ ]
- [ ]
- [ ]
- [ ]

4-WEEKS PRIOR

- [ ]
- [ ]
- [ ]
- [ ]
- [ ]
- [ ]
- [ ]

2-WEEKS PRIOR

- [ ]
- [ ]
- [ ]
- [ ]
- [ ]

MOVING DAY *Planner*

WEEK OF MOVE

- [ ]
- [ ]
- [ ]
- [ ]
- [ ]
- [ ]
- [ ]
- [ ]

MOVING DAY

- [ ]
- [ ]
- [ ]
- [ ]
- [ ]
- [ ]

NOTES & REMINDERS

IMPORTANT DATES

Month

Notes

MOVING BOX *Inventory*

ROOM: BOX NO: COLOR CODE:

CONTENTS:

ROOM: BOX NO: COLOR CODE:

CONTENTS:

ROOM: BOX NO: COLOR CODE:

CONTENTS:

ROOM: BOX NO: COLOR CODE:

CONTENTS:

MOVING BOX *Inventory*

ROOM: BOX NO: COLOR CODE:

CONTENTS:

ROOM: BOX NO: COLOR CODE:

CONTENTS:

ROOM: BOX NO: COLOR CODE:

CONTENTS:

ROOM: BOX NO: COLOR CODE:

CONTENTS:

MOVING BOX *Inventory*

ROOM: BOX NO: COLOR CODE:

CONTENTS:

ROOM: BOX NO: COLOR CODE:

CONTENTS:

ROOM: BOX NO: COLOR CODE:

CONTENTS:

ROOM: BOX NO: COLOR CODE:

CONTENTS:

MOVING BOX *Inventory*

ROOM: BOX NO: COLOR CODE:

CONTENTS:

ROOM: BOX NO: COLOR CODE:

CONTENTS:

ROOM: BOX NO: COLOR CODE:

CONTENTS:

ROOM: BOX NO: COLOR CODE:

CONTENTS:

MOVING BOX *Inventory*

ROOM: BOX NO: COLOR CODE:

CONTENTS:

ROOM: BOX NO: COLOR CODE:

CONTENTS:

ROOM: BOX NO: COLOR CODE:

CONTENTS:

ROOM: BOX NO: COLOR CODE:

CONTENTS:

MOVING BOX *Inventory*

ROOM: | BOX NO: | COLOR CODE:

CONTENTS:

ROOM: | BOX NO: | COLOR CODE:

CONTENTS:

ROOM: | BOX NO: | COLOR CODE:

CONTENTS:

ROOM: | BOX NO: | COLOR CODE:

CONTENTS:

MOVING BOX *Inventory*

ROOM: BOX NO: COLOR CODE:

CONTENTS:

ROOM: BOX NO: COLOR CODE:

CONTENTS:

ROOM: BOX NO: COLOR CODE:

CONTENTS:

ROOM: BOX NO: COLOR CODE:

CONTENTS:

MOVING BOX *Inventory*

ROOM: | BOX NO: | COLOR CODE:

CONTENTS:

ROOM: | BOX NO: | COLOR CODE:

CONTENTS:

ROOM: | BOX NO: | COLOR CODE:

CONTENTS:

ROOM: | BOX NO: | COLOR CODE:

CONTENTS:

MOVING BOX *Inventory*

ROOM: BOX NO: COLOR CODE:

CONTENTS:

ROOM: BOX NO: COLOR CODE:

CONTENTS:

ROOM: BOX NO: COLOR CODE:

CONTENTS:

ROOM: BOX NO: COLOR CODE:

CONTENTS:

MOVING BOX *Inventory*

ROOM: BOX NO: COLOR CODE:

CONTENTS:

ROOM: BOX NO: COLOR CODE:

CONTENTS:

ROOM: BOX NO: COLOR CODE:

CONTENTS:

ROOM: BOX NO: COLOR CODE:

CONTENTS:

MOVING BOX *Inventory*

ROOM: BOX NO: COLOR CODE:

CONTENTS:

ROOM: BOX NO: COLOR CODE:

CONTENTS:

ROOM: BOX NO: COLOR CODE:

CONTENTS:

ROOM: BOX NO: COLOR CODE:

CONTENTS:

MOVING BOX *Inventory*

ROOM: BOX NO: COLOR CODE:

CONTENTS:

ROOM: BOX NO: COLOR CODE:

CONTENTS:

ROOM: BOX NO: COLOR CODE:

CONTENTS:

ROOM: BOX NO: COLOR CODE:

CONTENTS:

MOVING BOX *Inventory*

ROOM: BOX NO: COLOR CODE:

CONTENTS:

ROOM: BOX NO: COLOR CODE:

CONTENTS:

ROOM: BOX NO: COLOR CODE:

CONTENTS:

ROOM: BOX NO: COLOR CODE:

CONTENTS:

MOVING BOX *Inventory*

ROOM: | BOX NO: | COLOR CODE:

CONTENTS:

ROOM: | BOX NO: | COLOR CODE:

CONTENTS:

ROOM: | BOX NO: | COLOR CODE:

CONTENTS:

ROOM: | BOX NO: | COLOR CODE:

CONTENTS:

MOVING BOX *Inventory*

ROOM: | BOX NO: | COLOR CODE:

CONTENTS:

ROOM: | BOX NO: | COLOR CODE:

CONTENTS:

ROOM: | BOX NO: | COLOR CODE:

CONTENTS:

ROOM: | BOX NO: | COLOR CODE:

CONTENTS:

MOVING BOX *Inventory*

ROOM:	BOX NO:	COLOR CODE:

CONTENTS:

ROOM:	BOX NO:	COLOR CODE:

CONTENTS:

ROOM:	BOX NO:	COLOR CODE:

CONTENTS:

ROOM:	BOX NO:	COLOR CODE:

CONTENTS:

MOVING BOX *Inventory*

ROOM: BOX NO: COLOR CODE:

CONTENTS:

ROOM: BOX NO: COLOR CODE:

CONTENTS:

ROOM: BOX NO: COLOR CODE:

CONTENTS:

ROOM: BOX NO: COLOR CODE:

CONTENTS:

MOVING BOX *Inventory*

ROOM: BOX NO: COLOR CODE:

CONTENTS:

ROOM: BOX NO: COLOR CODE:

CONTENTS:

ROOM: BOX NO: COLOR CODE:

CONTENTS:

ROOM: BOX NO: COLOR CODE:

CONTENTS:

ROOM *Planner*

ROOM:

PAINT COLORS::

COLOR SCHEME:

DÉCOR IDEAS:

FURNITURE IDEAS:

NOTES:

ROOM:

PAINT COLORS::

COLOR SCHEME:

DÉCOR IDEAS:

FURNITURE IDEAS:

NOTES:

NEW ROOM *Planner*

ROOM:

PAINT COLORS::

COLOR CODE:

DÉCOR IDEAS:

FURNITURE IDEAS:

THINGS TO DO:

- [ ]
- [ ]
- [ ]
- [ ]
- [ ]
- [ ]
- [ ]
- [ ]
- [ ]
- [ ]
- [ ]

DÉCOR IDEAS:

ROOM *Planner*

ROOM:

PAINT COLORS::

COLOR SCHEME:

DÉCOR IDEAS:

FURNITURE IDEAS:

NOTES:

ROOM:

PAINT COLORS::

COLOR SCHEME:

DÉCOR IDEAS:

FURNITURE IDEAS:

NOTES:

NEW ROOM *Planner*

ROOM:

PAINT COLORS::

COLOR CODE:

DÉCOR IDEAS:

FURNITURE IDEAS:

THINGS TO DO:

- [ ]
- [ ]
- [ ]
- [ ]
- [ ]
- [ ]
- [ ]
- [ ]
- [ ]
- [ ]

DÉCOR IDEAS:

ROOM *Planner*

ROOM:

PAINT COLORS::

COLOR SCHEME:

DÉCOR IDEAS:

FURNITURE IDEAS:

NOTES:

ROOM:

PAINT COLORS::

COLOR SCHEME:

DÉCOR IDEAS:

FURNITURE IDEAS:

NOTES:

NEW ROOM *Planner*

ROOM:

PAINT COLORS::

COLOR CODE:

DÉCOR IDEAS:

FURNITURE IDEAS:

THINGS TO DO:

- [ ]
- [ ]
- [ ]
- [ ]
- [ ]
- [ ]
- [ ]
- [ ]
- [ ]
- [ ]
- [ ]

DÉCOR IDEAS:

ROOM *Planner*

ROOM:

PAINT COLORS::

COLOR SCHEME:

DÉCOR IDEAS:

FURNITURE IDEAS:

NOTES:

ROOM:

PAINT COLORS::

COLOR SCHEME:

DÉCOR IDEAS:

FURNITURE IDEAS:

NOTES:

NEW ROOM *Planner*

ROOM:

PAINT COLORS::

COLOR CODE:

DÉCOR IDEAS:

FURNITURE IDEAS:

THINGS TO DO:

- [ ]
- [ ]
- [ ]
- [ ]
- [ ]
- [ ]
- [ ]
- [ ]
- [ ]
- [ ]
- [ ]

DÉCOR IDEAS:

ROOM *Planner*

ROOM:

PAINT COLORS::

COLOR SCHEME:

DÉCOR IDEAS:

FURNITURE IDEAS:

NOTES:

ROOM:

PAINT COLORS::

COLOR SCHEME:

DÉCOR IDEAS:

FURNITURE IDEAS:

NOTES:

NEW ROOM *Planner*

ROOM:

PAINT COLORS::

COLOR CODE:

DÉCOR IDEAS:

FURNITURE IDEAS:

THINGS TO DO:

- [ ]
- [ ]
- [ ]
- [ ]
- [ ]
- [ ]
- [ ]
- [ ]
- [ ]
- [ ]
- [ ]

DÉCOR IDEAS:

ROOM *Planner*

ROOM:

PAINT COLORS::

COLOR SCHEME:

DÉCOR IDEAS:

FURNITURE IDEAS:

NOTES:

ROOM:

PAINT COLORS::

COLOR SCHEME:

DÉCOR IDEAS:

FURNITURE IDEAS:

NOTES:

NEW ROOM *Planner*

ROOM:

PAINT COLORS::

COLOR CODE:

DÉCOR IDEAS:

FURNITURE IDEAS:

THINGS TO DO:

- [ ]
- [ ]
- [ ]
- [ ]
- [ ]
- [ ]
- [ ]
- [ ]
- [ ]
- [ ]
- [ ]

DÉCOR IDEAS:

ROOM *Planner*

ROOM:

PAINT COLORS::

COLOR SCHEME:

DÉCOR IDEAS:

FURNITURE IDEAS:

NOTES:

ROOM:

PAINT COLORS::

COLOR SCHEME:

DÉCOR IDEAS:

FURNITURE IDEAS:

NOTES:

NEW ROOM *Planner*

ROOM:

PAINT COLORS::

COLOR CODE:

DÉCOR IDEAS:

FURNITURE IDEAS:

THINGS TO DO:

- [ ]
- [ ]
- [ ]
- [ ]
- [ ]
- [ ]
- [ ]
- [ ]
- [ ]
- [ ]
- [ ]

DÉCOR IDEAS:

ROOM *Planner*

ROOM:

PAINT COLORS::

COLOR SCHEME:

DÉCOR IDEAS:

FURNITURE IDEAS:

NOTES:

ROOM:

PAINT COLORS::

COLOR SCHEME:

DÉCOR IDEAS:

FURNITURE IDEAS:

NOTES:

NEW ROOM *Planner*

ROOM:

PAINT COLORS::

COLOR CODE:

DÉCOR IDEAS:

FURNITURE IDEAS:

THINGS TO DO:

☐
☐
☐
☐
☐
☐
☐
☐
☐
☐
☐

DÉCOR IDEAS:

ROOM *Planner*

ROOM:

PAINT COLORS::

COLOR SCHEME:

DÉCOR IDEAS:

FURNITURE IDEAS:

NOTES:

ROOM:

PAINT COLORS::

COLOR SCHEME:

DÉCOR IDEAS:

FURNITURE IDEAS:

NOTES:

NEW ROOM *Planner*

ROOM:

PAINT COLORS::

COLOR CODE:

DÉCOR IDEAS:

FURNITURE IDEAS:

THINGS TO DO:

- [ ]
- [ ]
- [ ]
- [ ]
- [ ]
- [ ]
- [ ]
- [ ]
- [ ]
- [ ]
- [ ]

DÉCOR IDEAS:

ROOM *Planner*

ROOM:

PAINT COLORS::

COLOR SCHEME:

DÉCOR IDEAS:

FURNITURE IDEAS:

NOTES:

ROOM:

PAINT COLORS::

COLOR SCHEME:

DÉCOR IDEAS:

FURNITURE IDEAS:

NOTES:

NEW ROOM *Planner*

ROOM:

PAINT COLORS::

COLOR CODE:

DÉCOR IDEAS:

FURNITURE IDEAS:

THINGS TO DO:

- [ ]
- [ ]
- [ ]
- [ ]
- [ ]
- [ ]
- [ ]
- [ ]
- [ ]
- [ ]
- [ ]

DÉCOR IDEAS:

ROOM *Planner*

ROOM:

PAINT COLORS::

COLOR SCHEME:

DÉCOR IDEAS:

FURNITURE IDEAS:

NOTES:

ROOM:

PAINT COLORS::

COLOR SCHEME:

DÉCOR IDEAS:

FURNITURE IDEAS:

NOTES:

NEW ROOM *Planner*

ROOM:

PAINT COLORS::

COLOR CODE:

DÉCOR IDEAS:

FURNITURE IDEAS:

THINGS TO DO:

- [ ]
- [ ]
- [ ]
- [ ]
- [ ]
- [ ]
- [ ]
- [ ]
- [ ]
- [ ]
- [ ]

DÉCOR IDEAS:

ROOM *Planner*

ROOM:

PAINT COLORS::

COLOR SCHEME:

DÉCOR IDEAS:

FURNITURE IDEAS:

NOTES:

ROOM:

PAINT COLORS::

COLOR SCHEME:

DÉCOR IDEAS:

FURNITURE IDEAS:

NOTES:

NEW ROOM *Planner*

ROOM:

PAINT COLORS::

COLOR CODE:

DÉCOR IDEAS:

FURNITURE IDEAS:

THINGS TO DO:

- [ ]
- [ ]
- [ ]
- [ ]
- [ ]
- [ ]
- [ ]
- [ ]
- [ ]
- [ ]
- [ ]

DÉCOR IDEAS:

ROOM *Planner*

ROOM:

PAINT COLORS::

COLOR SCHEME:

DÉCOR IDEAS:

FURNITURE IDEAS:

NOTES:

ROOM:

PAINT COLORS::

COLOR SCHEME:

DÉCOR IDEAS:

FURNITURE IDEAS:

NOTES:

NEW ROOM *Planner*

ROOM:

PAINT COLORS::

COLOR CODE:

DÉCOR IDEAS:

FURNITURE IDEAS:

THINGS TO DO:

- [ ]
- [ ]
- [ ]
- [ ]
- [ ]
- [ ]
- [ ]
- [ ]
- [ ]
- [ ]
- [ ]

DÉCOR IDEAS:

Enyoing this book?
Please leave a review. I would be happy
to receive a feedback and your opinion.

Thanks for your support.

Made in the USA
Monee, IL
09 June 2021